Maria Anne Hirschmann

Hansi
Shares
How You Can
Face the Future
Without Fear

Are You Prepared?

Hansi
BOOKS

HANSI MINISTRIES, INC.
P.O. BOX 552 HUNTINGTON BEACH, CA 92648

Scripture quotations in this publication are from the Authorized King James Version. Also quoted are:

NASB New American Standard Bible. © The Lockman Foundation 1960, 1962, 1963, 1971. Used by permission.

RSV Revised Standard Version of the Bible, copyrighted 1946 and 1952 by the Division of Christian Education of the NCCC, U.S.A., and used by permission.

Published by Hansi Ministries, Inc.
Huntington Beach, California 92648
Printed in U.S.A.

Library of Congress Catalog Card No. 79- 90957
ISBN 0-932878-06-7

Contents

1. The Reason Why

People who have read my book every so often come to me and say, "Hansi, if our country should ever face some hard times, I hope I have you around. You would know what to do at such times. You have lived through them before!"

I've thought a lot about it and tried to understand what they meant. I also talked to God and asked Him to give me wisdom and insight about my past, the present and the future. I wondered for a long time how my experiences of a poverty-ridden, harsh childhood and youth, my austere life in Nazi training, my trials in a Communist labor camp, or as a refugee could benefit people in an affluent society such as we have in our Western world.

God gave me a glimpse of an answer in the last decade when I began to see every symptom of Nazi Germany raise its ugly head here in America. The Lord sent me out to speak up across the land and to warn my fellow Americans about the danger of losing democracy and freedom in the years to come and to suggest a solution to them.

Lately, I carry a new burden on my heart. Troubled times for America and the entire world are not only a possibility

5

anymore, they are becoming a surety—and in the near future. It is hard to face the fact that our Christian nation will most likely not be willing to heed God's admonitions any longer. And what we are not willing to learn in good times, we might have to learn under hardship. That is nothing new. The entire Old Testament of the Bible tells that story. Obedience to God brings heavenly blessings and protections. Ignoring God's rules brings hardship and suffering. We *do* know that God's judgments can be reversed or delayed for the Bible says that also (see Zephaniah 3:15; Jonah 3:10).

I do not know *what* the future holds for my beloved United States; I am not a prophet. But I do know by now, for sure, that it will take supernatural intervention and a miracle to stop our nation from going where it is headed: toward financial disaster, more and more government control, loss of individual freedom and a takeover by either socialism or some form of dictatorship. Things change so rapidly that it is hard to predict when and if a crash might come. Dangers could sneak up on us secretly, as they have so far and people will suddenly wake up to a morning when America's democracy and freedom are gone.

I do know I am not afraid. I do not know what my future holds, but I *do* know *Who* holds my future. That is enough for me (see Psalm 47; Matthew 6:25–34)!

My great concern is for my unprepared American neighbors, especially my brothers and sisters in God's family. The prophet Hosea lamented: "My people are destroyed for lack of knowledge" (Hosea 4:6).

People can bring unnecessary hardship and frustration upon themselves by trying to ignore what appears unpleasant and refusing to prepare themselves for it. They tend to say, "It could not happen to us." However, this rationalizing will not keep things from happening, just as one does not keep a tornado away by refusing to build a storm shelter.

I believe that God wants us to build storm shelters *right*

now on three levels: spiritual, mental and physical. Having faith in His care and protection does not mean that we stick our heads in the sand and refuse to think things through. God will never do for us what we can do ourselves. He wants us to be "wise as serpents, and harmless as doves" (Matthew 10:16). For Christians it is often easier to be harmless than to become wise.

I have done a lot of praying and meditating lately. I know and can see some things that you, my fellow Americans, cannot see yet, because you have always lived in a land of freedom and plenty. By the time the troubles are visible to everyone, it will be hard to do something about it. It is impossible to build a storm shelter when the tornado is ready to touch down. Think how many lives have been lost in times past because people ignored the warning and did not prepare for the storm, or neglected to enter the shelter after they built it!

Remember that everything else on earth that you lose can be replaced except life and health itself. I know that firsthand because I watched property, wealth and positions vanish after World War II in Europe. I had none of these but I lost my health and almost my life and sanity in the terrible struggle for physical and emotional survival. God kept me alive and has restored me through the years here in America. I thank Him for it. He taught me many things.

I wish I had learned faster, for then I could have avoided many hardships which I thought God had "sent" to me. He didn't send them. My ignorance brought the problems on and He graciously pulled me through. I carry many scars today, but with them came insights.

I don't have any magic formula for the future, and I do not claim to know it all. But I want to share how things look to me on three levels—spiritual, mental and physical. If what I say makes sense to you, apply it. If not, perhaps you have greater insights. All I want to do is give what I have and pray that it might help many to prepare for the storm of these last days before Jesus comes. We can face the future without fear, for we Christians *have* a shelter. Isn't it time we learned *how* to use it?

In my first booklet, *If My People,* I shared my thoughts about our responsibility toward our community and our country. This little book talks about our personal responsibilities toward ourselves and our own families.

Storms are never easy, but you are not without a choice. You may either sit there and let yourself be blown to pieces—or you may use strong wings like an eagle. He rides on top of a storm—higher and higher, and ever closer to blue sky and God's presence.

_____

Now that you have read this chapter, you need to reflect and think it through for yourself. Please, take the time to find the following Bible verses:

The storm: 2 Timothy 2:1–14

Not too late: Zephaniah 3:15; Jonah 3:4–10

Your shelter: Psalm 61:1–4; John 10:27–29

Your assurance: Psalm 47; Matthew 6:25–34

God's will for you to choose: Isaiah 40:31;
     Romans 8:35–39

In a small notebook write down in your own words what God is telling *you* in this chapter and what you are planning to do about your new convictions!

2. *Are You Afraid?*

Are you afraid? If someone asked *you* that question, what would you answer? Would you say: "Of course, I'm not, because as a Christian, I know that God takes care of me!" Or would you be totally honest and, though knowing what you are supposed to say as a "positive" Christian, admit, "Yes, I am afraid though I should not be. I wonder what would happen if my steady income was cut off. What would happen to my children's future?..."

I shall never forget the night when I went to the Lord utterly discouraged. I had spoken that evening to a large community group, many of whom had been in one of my meetings just a year before. At that first meeting I had poured out my heart about my deep concern for America and asked them to start praying for our land every day. Now I asked for a show of hands of those who had been praying and not more than three or four hands were raised.

I crawled into my unfamiliar hotel bed completely defeated. "Lord," I cried, "what sense does it make that I spend most of my time traveling, speaking or writing when other people of my age have settled down toward a rocking chair and retirement? Why is it so hard to wake up the Christians to the great dangers that lie ahead? It almost seems that the Body of Christ as a whole is paralyzed. What is the cause?"

God's answer came back immediately and so clearly that it hit me like a bolt of lightning. "The children of God are paralyzed by the spirit of fear!"

I didn't sleep much for the rest of the night. I did much meditating, praying and searching. How much fear did *I* carry? Why was fear so devastating? Where did fear begin?

It all started when Adam sinned. The very first sentence he said after he had disobeyed God and hid from the Lord's presence was, "I heard thy voice...and I was afraid" (Genesis 3:10). As soon as the newly created earth-children of God got in disharmony with their Creator, Satan took over and he brought fear into every human life. By it he bound every human being because sin brings death.

But we read in the Epistle to the Hebrews that Christ came to "destroy him that had the power of death, that is, the devil; and deliver them who through fear of death were all their lifetime subject to bondage" (Hebrews 2:14,15). Jesus Christ came to deliver those who believe in Him from that fear of death which *is* the root of any other fear a person can be plagued by. You say, "Sure, I *should* look forward to dying because I am going to be with the Lord, like Paul said (see 2 Corinthians 5:6–8). I am going home, I know, but I ain't homesick yet!"

I don't think that God's children need to be eager to die, but is it God's will to be as filled with fears as we are? Fear is Satan's greatest weapon to destroy our joy, peace and effectiveness for God's cause and the good we could do for our country's sake.

We carry fear on all three levels of our humanness. Our body carries our soul and spirit, therefore our physical-survival instinct pressures us the hardest. To wonder what we

10

will eat tomorrow, where we would live if we couldn't make our mortgage payments any longer, or how to clothe ourselves if the stores had nothing on the shelves, are valid concerns and deserve our sensible attention. We need to think things through, make provisions the best we can—and tell any fears which beset us after that to get lost.

People without God often carry less fears than God's children do. Why? Because Satan, their father, the author of fear, knows that the godless *should* be in fear, for the *fear* of God is the beginning of wisdom (see Proverbs 9:10). But Satan shields his own from godly fear so that he can hold them in bondage.

The world needs to fear God and death and hopefully be brought by that fear to see the need of a Saviour and salvation from eternal death. That is the beginning! Then, as soon as a person is led by a healthy fear of judgment and God's punishment to make peace with God, that fear must go and be replaced by love. We cannot *scare* each other into heaven. As we become united in the Body of Christ, God wants us to *love* Him and one another and to grow together as a family.

God knows that the devil uses fear more than anything else to torture the Body of Christ, just as Satan harassed the children of Israel, according to the Old Testament records. The devil brought fear on the Israelites and caused their exodus to halt for a whole generation (see Numbers 13:27; 14:35). They lived and died in the wilderness. They never saw the Promised Land, not because it was God's will but because they chose to listen to their fears instead of to God through Moses. Caleb in his speech to Joshua reminded him: "Nevertheless my brethren (eight out of ten spies) that went up with me made the heart of the people (God's people, not the heathen) melt (with fear): but I wholly followed the Lord my God" (Joshua 14:8).

Caleb and Joshua were the only two people in their generation to reach Canaan because they were not afraid. Could fear keep some people out of heaven? I am sure that some people will miss heaven because they were completely subject to fear rather than a great vice. John tells us in his Revelation that "the *fearful,* and unbelieving, and the abominable, and murderers, and whoremongers, and sorcerers, and idolators, and all liars, shall have their part in the lake which burneth with fire and brimstone: which is the second death" (Revelation 21:8). The fearful are mentioned first, ahead of other great wickedness!

God uses a great economy of words in the Bible. He had to in order to put everything we need to know about the past, present and future of our world into *one* book. Yet, God saw it necessary to repeat the phrases "fear not" and "be not afraid" ninety-six times in the Word of God.

He foresaw that the world would run carelessly to its doom and when fear would finally seize the people they wouldn't know how to undo their course to perdition. We are told that at the end of time many calamities will befall this earth: "And there shall be signs in the sun, and in the moon, and in the stars; and upon the earth distress of nations, with perplexity; the sea and the waves roaring; *men's hearts failing them for fear,* and for looking after those things which are coming on the earth" (Luke 21:25,26).

Could it be more than an accident that the number one killer in the Western hemisphere is heart failure? You say, "Not everybody who died of a heart attack was a bundle of fears."

No, maybe not; he or she suffered from stress instead. And stress kills people in a hundred ways! Fear has many names or forms and often noble disguises! We are not only afraid of death or getting hurt or being left alone or rejected, we carry fear of fear itself and worry whether we are really saved. Fear's twin sister is guilt. How often we sit in God's presence paralyzed by guilt, afraid to accept His limitless love, peace and all encompassing forgiveness.

Are you afraid? Look into your heart. Is Jesus Christ your Saviour? If you invited Him to come in and take over, you have eternal life right now (see John 5:24). Through His blood you were born into the family of God (see John 1:12). Who is your Father? The King of the universe who made heaven and earth! And He owns all the silver and gold and the cattle on a thousand hills (see Haggai 2:8; Psalm 50:10,11).

Does the future look forbidding? It should to the world and hopefully it will bring some people around to seek God. But Christians have a shelter if we want to use it; read Psalm 91. The only problem is that our fears paralyze us so much that we forget to enter and use it.

You say you cannot shake your fears regardless of how hard you try? Maybe you haven't learned to do it God's way. Jesus has told us that fear is a spirit not sent by God. Paul wrote to his young friend Timothy, who couldn't help but battle fears in the turmoil of his time: "For God hath not given us the spirit of fear; but (the spirit) of power, and of love, and of a sound mind" (2 Timothy 1:7).

A spirit not given by God is an evil spirit or a demon. Jesus has shown us how to get rid of demons. They have to be commanded to leave in the name of Jesus. The disciples did it (see Luke 10:17) and this power is not the exclusive property of any denomination; neither should it be claimed or rejected as a "charismatic" doctrine. This is old-time, simple gospel truth and existed long before our hairsplitting arguments of doctrine existed. It is so simple that it offends our sophisticated Western thinking. But it works. At least it works for me. When any fear creeps into me and I find myself in a state of anxiety, unrest, foreboding or depression, I say aloud—because the devil cannot read my thoughts: "Spirit of fear (guilt, depression) you must leave now in Jesus' name. God, my Father in heaven has prepared a place for you. I command you and I bind you, Satan, in the name and by the blood of my Lord Jesus Christ. Amen."

13

If the spirit of fear comes back, I repeat my command until Satan gets the message. After he realizes that I mean it, and I resist as long as it takes, he flees (see James 4:7). Satan can hear the name of Jesus just so long and then he has to run. The monkey of fear never leaves his back. He knows what's waiting for him and he seeks to lead as many as possible into the position he is in—away from life, contentment, joy and the peace we have in God.

After the spirit of fear has been commanded to leave, I ask Jesus to fill the vacuum with His spirit of power, love and a sound mind (see 2 Timothy 1:7). If we leave the place empty, the fear demon will come back and move in again, bringing seven more evil spirits along with him (see Matthew 12:43–45).

The choice is ours. God will not stop the fears or force you and me to trust Him instead. We all have His gift of freedom of choice. By that freedom we may choose to live either in peace and without constant fear or to agonize through the wilderness of life and finally die of heart failure or other stress disease.

Satan is a liar, the father of every lie that ever was said on earth. His fears are lies, too. And Jesus came not only to deliver us from death and eternal absence from God, but from every lie: the lies that make us fear and tremble. Nobody who knows Christ needs to be afraid—unless he *wants* to. Why would you want to?

Consider the fears that plague us. Here is a list of some of them and some Scriptures that answer them. Add other verses that the Lord gives you. Write the antidote for each fear in your notebook. Add to the list fears you may have and find an answer for them is the Bible. You will need a concordance for your search.

14

Fear	*Scripture*
Fear of death	John 11:25
Fear of poverty	Philippians 4:19
Fear of sickness	2 Corinthians 12:8,9
Fear of rejection	John 15:15,16
Fear of being alone	Joshua 1:5; Hebrews 13:5
Fear of failure	Romans 8:37; Philippians 4:13
Fear of judgment	Romans 8:1
Fear of failing God	2 Corinthians 9:8
Fear of fear	I John 4:18

3. A Strong Spirit

A Christian functions on three levels. (See *I Am But a Child in Christ,* chapters 2,3,4.) We have a body, soul and spirit. God through Paul placed these levels of function the other way around: "Now may the God of peace Himself sanctify you entirely; and may your spirit and soul and body be preserved complete" *NASB;* or, as *RSV* puts it, "be kept sound and blameless" (I Thessalonians 5:23).

When we are spiritually reborn and enter God's family, our spirit life begins in the newborn or baby stage. It has to compete with our soul and body which are much older. Nevertheless, God wants His children to grow spiritually and be more and more guided by the spirit and not by the soul and body. Why is it so important to let our spirit grow, mature and become strong?

First of all, it is the spirit who will guide us toward eternity and heavenly values. And a strong human spirit will help us to survive and triumph over insurmountable difficulties on earth. The right human spirit is in the long run stronger than armies, atomic bombs, hunger, pestilence, freezing cold or scorching heat. We see this when we look at our own country's history. How did our country of freedom and democracy begin? The courageous spirit of a handful of settlers, who trusted God and their own destiny, faced an overpowering army that was well clothed and well fed. Hungry, freezing, clad in rags, with only a few arms but an unconquerable spirit, our forefathers drove the oppressors out and set up freedom and independence. They were led by a general who wasn't ashamed to kneel on the frozen soil of the battlefield, pleading with God for help, and who took his own coat to wrap around a shivering soldier standing watch at night.

A strong human spirit, linked with the Spirit of God, can do the impossible. Why? Because the things of the spirit are the *true* realities. God is a Spirit. He is the only reality who always existed, never changes and never disappears. The physical and material matters on this earth are subject to constant change and disappear readily. There is no constant for us in the physical realm. Therefore, the physical will and must always be submissive to the spiritual.

If your human spirit is to be of help to you, it must be strong. But, prepare yourself for conflict if you intend to build a strong spirit by the aid of God's Spirit. Your body will yell and have fits. Your soul will reason that you are foolish and will demand that you abide by habits that are already deeply ingrained and provide the material securities you have trusted in for so long.

God has certain principles and rules for His earth children to live by if they want to be strong and healthy. These principles are: *clean air, exercise,* plenty of pure *water* and enough *food*. These principles must be applied to all three levels of function: spiritual, mental and emotional or physical.

Clean Air

The human body can survive only four minutes without air. What is the clean air of our spirit? The presence of God and His Spirit in the form of spiritual power, love, forgiveness and many others. Without these, the spirit cannot survive.

18

What is the foul air? The evil spirits of fear, guilt, hate, unforgiveness and legions of others.

How can we provide a clean environment for our spirits? By commanding in Christ's power and name, that the evil spirits leave and then asking God to give us His Spirit instead. Sounds too simple, doesn't it? Have you ever tried it? If you do you might find a strange thing happening. You may suddenly think: "Okay, Lord, I want to get rid of everything evil and receive your gifts, *but*—that *one* person I cannot forgive and I am not so sure I should. I am willing to give up everything evil *but* that *one* special little sin or pleasure I would like to keep. I will let you do anything with me and my life *but* I refuse to ever be alone. I trust everything to you *but* don't ever take away my home (family, job, position, savings account, etc., etc.)."

Exercise

As soon as you find your soul and body objecting with "if" or "but," then you will discover that you must decide whether to exercise spiritually or not. Spiritual exercise (as any exercise) is not so much based on flexing your muscles and keeping them tight as on relaxing and letting go. (More details are in the next chapter.) One of the strongest spiritual laws that exists is: What we hold on to we lose. What we give up and let go, we gain and receive back (see Matthew 16:25,26; Mark 8:35-37; Luke 9:24,25). God put Himself under that principle when He gave all He had to give, without withholding anything back to save us from eternal separation from Him (see John 3:16,17,36; Galatians 4:4,5).

We "let go" of our old life to receive new, eternal life; but the rule must also be applied in everyday life and on every level of living. We hold on to another person too tightly and we lose what we love—be it our mate, children or friends. Nobody wants to be put into a straitjacket, not even in the name of love.

19

We wrap our main attention around material possessions and find ourselves suddenly alone with a pile of junk. The most expensive car or our house can fall apart or be destroyed within seconds.

We preoccupy ourselves with our own physical or soul needs to the point where we bring on by our own fears what we are afraid of. Remember, we are and we become what we think. "As (a man) thinketh in his heart, so is he" (Proverbs 23:7). Or, we can, even in a faltering little baby step, hand to God all we are and think and want, in an exercise of trust and faith. We "let go!" We must do it over and over. Walking is not one single and final step but walking is done step after step, move after move.

Water and Food

We need spiritual water and food. As the human body can exist only four days without water and forty to sixty days without food, our spirit can exist only in the presence of life always and communication with God constantly.

The watering of our spirit is done by prayer. I do not talk about the "official" church prayers and the blessing at meals, as important as such forms and habits may be. I talk about two-way communication between you and heaven. Many of us wait until we are in trouble before we talk to God, but if you forget in good times to communicate with God, how will you know how to call on Him and hear Him in hard times.

Learn to talk to Jesus as a friend not only when you need Him, but at all times. How often do you tell God that you love Him when things are going right for you? How often does He get the credit when you make a smart move? How much praise fills your praying?

Food for the spirit is the Word of God. I know what you think: "I simply don't have the time to study. Furthermore, I am not the studious type."

Well, who is studious when it comes to spiritual food?

Nobody is born with a natural appetite for the "right" spiritual food! We are all born with an inclination toward sin and the "wrong" stuff which leads to decay and death on three levels. Good habits don't come by instinct, they are developed. Appetite for the "right" foods grow as we learn to eat them. Begin with small bits if you have spiritual indigestion. Everyone has time enough to read one Bible text a day (or evening). Ask the Lord to show you what He is trying to say to you about your study of His Word. Think it through, let it sink in.

When hard times come, the Holy Spirit will recall the spiritual truths that have submerged into your subconscious mind. But if your mind has not been adequately exposed to God's Word, how can even God recall what isn't there?

As our body builds reserves from good food which can pull us through in times of starvation, so a well-fed spirit has plenty to give in times of stress and suffering when the heavens seem shut. We should not go to extremes and provide too much food for our physical bodies; but I doubt that any of us ever could expose ourselves to too much spiritual food and water. We must learn to talk to God like our best friend and to eat an abundance of His Word, or at least take a spiritual vitamin every day—one passage of Scripture and one short prayer session. It might save a life—and it could be yours!

Read the Scriptures suggested below. What are you planning to do about the needs of your spirit? Write it down in your notebook!

Clean air: Philippians 4:6,7
Pure water: Philippians 4:6,7
Healthful food: Psalm 19:7-10
Good exercise: Psalm 62:8
Add some verses that mean much to you.

4. A Balanced Soul

Of our three parts—spirit, soul and body—God sees our spirit as our innermost self, our "heart." He sees our soul as our individual self, the level that makes us a conscious being. Our human soul carries our intellect, our emotions and our will. Balance is necessary if we are to be "kept sound and blameless" (1 Thessalonians 5:23, *RSV*).

God's Spirit aims toward balance and harmony. He would like to guide our will; our will, in turn, must balance emotions and intellect, body and soul. But God will not force His guidance on us. He created man with a freedom of choice. Each day He gives us many options, then He lets us choose as we will. Since freedom of choice underlies the human will, it therefore becomes the center of all three parts of our life—spirit, soul and body. We are free to decide either to let ourselves be controlled by our emotions, our cold intellect, our bodily needs and cravings or to let every avenue of our life be guided and balanced by the spirit.

What exercises do our souls need in order to become balanced?

/ *Exercise*

Satan is going to do all he can to cause imbalance and disharmony between the three parts of ourselves. He most often employs our emotions to play havoc with our nerves. Evil spirits use the avenue of our sensitive emotions to make us *feel* fear, guilt, hate and many other defense mechanisms. Even our love for another person can be threatened by our emotions if Satan is behind them. We often *feel* jealous, threatened, possessive or rejected in a love relationship.

So, since our emotions often seem to have a greater influence over our souls than intellect or will, perhaps we should consider emotional exercise.

Some people tend to be highly emotional—they go by urges, surges and purges of the body. Other people pride themselves on being able to lean on their own understanding and reasoning power. Neither way of thinking is helpful in times of crisis. The Spirit of God longs to turn our emotions around and make positive solid principles out of fickle feelings. For that we have to let our reasoning intellect (enlightened by the Spirit) look at our feelings and then we wisely "will" which ones we permit to influence our actions. In other words, we should not love, talk or act as we *feel* like it but as the Spirit shows us. (We would never forgive another person or ourselves if we depended on our feelings. We forgive with our will, regardless of how we feel.)

And we give our loved ones the same right to this freedom of choice because it is God's will for every human being. Even if we have to battle and cast out jealousy and suspicion, we don't let these bad spirits unbalance our lives and relationships.

You say: "It's easily said but much harder to put into practice!" That is true, but you will never come to the place where you *can* control your emotions unless you start the exercise of your will. And how will you control your runaway emotions in a true crisis if you haven't learned to balance

24

them with common sense and your will in good times?

God will always try to teach His children gently, only one step at a time. If we refuse to learn a lesson, He gives it back until we learn it. Every time a lesson comes back it is a bit harder. If we haven't learned it by the end of our lives, we often go through a "crash course" of final loneliness, sickness or other circumstances to learn to "let go" and to learn the trust that we need to step over the threshold of time into eternity.

If we are to prepare ourselves for the stormy times ahead, our emotions have to be controlled by our will and a mind that knows and trusts God. I have watched people around me go crazy and have a nervous breakdown both after World War II and even during peace times here in America, because they were so used to giving in to their emotions. Our emotions were given to us by God and are good, but you cannot allow them to guide you independent of your will. If you do, you are prone to panic or irrational behavior.

Which of your emotions do you consider "hot" or uncontrollable? The advice to count to ten before reacting when you are upset is old but good. I believe our present time needs a stronger version. Count to a hundred or more, especially if you are one who jumps into a car squealing out of your driveway with smoking tires when your emotions take control of your soul. "He who is slow to anger is better than the mighty" (Proverbs 16:32, *NASB*). "Let every one be quick to hear, slow to speak and slow to anger" (James 1:19, *NASB*).

You say, "Emotions are *not* my problem. I am analytical and make my decisions with cold hard logic in cold blood. My emotions are *never* running me!"

That is too bad, my friend. And I feel sorry for you and those around you. Nobody enjoys being around an iceberg and you might find yourself always *right* and often alone. Like those whose emotions drive them and others up a wall, you will drive others away with your insensitivity and in-

25

tellectual snobbishness. You need your emotions to be sensitive to yourself and those around you. And human beings were never meant to be computers, robots and calculators.

/ In times of hardship, you need the emotional ties of love and belonging to God, to yourself, to loved ones and to the soil you live on in order to have the will to survive. Your cold intellect can easily tell you that it is senseless to keep on going, and, unless you love life and others, you simply will give up the struggle. It is a well-known psychological fact that people who get lost in the wilderness, crash in a plane or are attacked by an incurable disease fight and often come out alive because they have an emotional reason for living.

If you feel embarrassed to ever show any emotion or a tear, ask God to set you free. Command Satan's spirit of bondage to leave. Smiles and tears are outlets of our soul. Keep both doors wide open! As you mingle your emotions with the principles of your intellect, let it be a tasteful mixture. The best soup is tasteless without salt or other seasonings. So season your emotions and intellect with positive honest feelings. You are never too young or too old to practice such soul exercises.

Clean Air

Be sure and exercise your soul in clean air! What is the "air" of the soul? Your pattern of thinking. Just as your body will not let you stop breathing—it's an involuntary action— so you cannot stop yourself from thinking, even in your sleep. You always have a thought in your thought channel, but you decide what *kind* of thought. Let your thoughts run wild and Satan will defile your imaginations and you will end up with a polluted soul. You might not always be able to control the intake of clean air into your lungs, but you always have a will to control the atmosphere of your soul. I often quote the saying, "You cannot stop the blackbirds from flying over your head, but you can stop them from nesting in your hair."

26

Your will decides if you are going to let evil thoughts spin and weave a trap for wrongdoings. You decide if you will play in your daydreaming with temptation, lust, murder, greed, wrong and covetousness or the good things that God wants you to think about. Nobody decides for you what you think—*ever*—unless you permit them!

If you permit the media (television, motion pictures, newspapers, magazines), music or other people to pattern your thinking without resistance, you will be easy prey tomorrow for the process of political and spiritual brainwashing. Hypnosis and the new forms of meditations (like Transcendental Meditation or similar kinds) will also break down your spiritual guard to your mind and your will. Beware of these. (See chapter 7 for further information.)

Remember, you have only two ways to direct your thinking. You either make a conscientious effort to hold up and to tune into God's wavelength or you let yourself slide—which always takes you down to the foul pits of hell. We have that natural inclination! To reverse the natural trend always takes effort. Evil habits and patterns develop in seconds. God and positive things take a long time and deliberate work.

Water and Food

The water for our soul is our interaction with God and others. No man is an island, and God said it is not good for men to be alone (see Genesis 2:18). We are social creatures. Some of us are extroverts, others draw inside. It does not matter as long as someone is there, wherever you turn. The outer interaction we cannot always control, but we decide when to interact with God. He is always there, waiting to water our thirsty soul. Too bad that we draw foul water so often from broken cisterns when we can have God and His companionship (see Jeremiah 2:13). We *never* are alone if we seek God. He always answers if we call. But He never forces Himself on us for companionship.

27

We also decide what food our soul takes in. We must make a deliberate effort to keep away from "junk food," both physically and for our soul. We here in America "nibble" ourselves sick, physically, emotionally and mentally. We permit our children to follow our wrong examples.

Who decides in your home what type of television or radio program may enter your souls—God, you or, worse yet, your inexperienced children or teenagers? If your children yell when you turn a bad program off, do you have any substitute for the junk food you are taking away? You must provide a satisfactory alternative for them.

If you wonder why your children never reach for a good book or refuse to listen to a good record or would rather go to a wild movie instead of spending an evening with you, ask yourself what "good food" do you offer so that they might learn to like it? Taste for good wholesome food must be acquired. It does not come naturally.

I read much to my children as they were growing up and often stopped in the middle of the story when it got very exciting. If they wanted to know the ending they had to read it themselves or read it to each other. Today my children read! If you are not a reader, start reading a good book one page at a time. It will grow on you, just like good music. The enjoyment of fine art, hobbies, doing or building things with your own hands and creating with a sense of beauty is worth the effort.

Time can someday become heavy and endless if you have not fed your soul in preparation for old age, or if you are depending on others to fill your soul! Inner resources of the soul need to be stored in good times just as full grainaries of the good years feed people in time of need. I shall never be afraid that my soul shall starve, as long as I have God—and a good book to read.

If today someone took your television and radio away, could your soul survive?

Again read the Scriptures and note God's answer to the needs of your soul. Write the teaching. Add verses of your own, if you desire.

Clean air: Philippians 4:8
Pure water: Hebrews 10:22-25
Healthful food: Philippians 3:19,20; Colossians 3:8
Good exercise: I Chronicles 28:9

5. *A Healthy Body*

People often ask me, "How do you stand all the pressures of traveling and speaking and stay well and slim at the same time? Are you a healthy type of person to whom such things come easily?

I answer, "No, I am not a healthy person by nature. I keep myself in shape and healthy by special efforts." When I proceed to tell them how, I get the funniest responses. Come to think of it, they are not funny, they are sad instead!

Many fellow Americans are willing to do anything but keep themselves in good physical condition. They would rather die—and they do. Hypertension and cancer are the two great killers in the Western world. Primitive cultures hardly know these two diseases. And if we want to avoid an untimely death by either of them, we had better watch what we do or don't do to bring them on.

The Bible tells us that we are fearfully and wonderfully made by our Creator (see Psalm 139:14). He not only put us together in a unique way, He also provided for our needs. Our physical body has to have air, water and food to sustain itself. God had clean air, pure water and nourishing food in His plan

31

for us when this world began. Somehow we humans managed to foul up God's plan, literally. Not too many of us who live in highly populated areas have a chance to breathe clean air. In addition, many people pollute their own and other people's air with tobacco smoke. I have talked to the Lord about it untold times and He showed me how to counteract what we cannot change.

Exercise

Though it would be foolish to over-exert yourself during a smog alert if you live in Los Angeles or any other smog-ridden city, it is most important to exercise. There are times when you can exercise, regardless of where you live. God *made* the human body for exercise just as much as our car manufacturers made cars for driving, not to sit motionless in a garage. Somehow, we oblige ourselves a lot more to the purposes of the auto industry than to God's original plan for us. I have said it often—as I say it now, daring to step on many toes by it—we Americans believe that God gave us two legs so we can push the gas pedal and the brakes in our vehicles. But He actually gave us our legs to walk with. What a shock! How many of our young people know that they can *walk* more than one city block?

Our body not only breathes through the nose and lungs but also through our skin. We need to take in a lot of clean air through all avenues to get enough oxygen into our system to function properly. As our lungs put the oxygen into our bloodstream, it is carried to every part of the body. Our brain receives the main share of it and needs it to "feel" right. If the lungs don't get enough of the life-giving oxygen, we end up oxygen starved. We feel fatigued, groggy, depressed, without pep, in need of rest, unable to cope with life. We blame God, the devil, others or our horoscope for our misery. And all the time what we need is a brisk walk to revive ourselves to a better life.

I do not know which exercise is best for you. I know what is most beneficial for me: walking. I cannot jog well. I have had three major surgeries and my sore bones refuse to submit to running. But I can walk, first slow and then in a stepped-up pace.

You say, "Well, maybe you *have* a place to walk, but I don't."

Listen, unless someone puts you in a straitjacket or ties you up, you can walk, even if it is in place in front of your open window. It's not as much fun as walking through the grass and under trees but it's better than nothing.

You say you have no time? We all have and make time for the things we consider important. If need be, cut your sleeping time. Thirty minutes shorter time in bed will add thirty minutes to your favorite form of exercise. I don't care if you swim, use a jump-rope, do gymnastics or run. Do it regularly. Your heart and life might depend on it.

You say, "I am not in the habit and I start out but I quit after a few days. Furthermore, my neighbors will think I am crazy if they see me walk around the block."

Well, if you are that self-conscious, get a dog. If you can't be kind to your own body, do it for the health of your pet. It's not so bad after all to go to the dogs—or with them.

I have found places for exercise all over the world. I talk to God about it and ask Him to find me a place to walk. I have walked the streets of big cities all over the world. I know many parks. One of my favorite places to walk is cemeteries. They are green and quiet. Tombstones tell fascinating stories. They also bring my tumbled worries quickly into proper perspective. Whatever gets me uptight, I look at the silent graves and think, "If this were my last day on earth, would I be upset about money (gossip, human conflicts, misunderstandings, administrational) problems?" It's a safe place to walk. Criminals don't lurk behind graves to slug me. They are usually where the money is.

When I am home, I walk at a nearby golf course. No, I don't play golf, but I do more walking than the golfers. They drive carts.

Walking is my favorite time to commune with God.

Water and Food

My next favorite place and time to commune with God is in a hot shower. I get my best thoughts for speaking and writing there.

Water is important not only to wash my "inner organs" but it's my number one therapy for keeping my dragging, ever sore body going. I have used water therapy as long as I can remember. As a child, I loved to walk barefoot over the pebbles in the ice-cold water of the creek, long before I learned that it was a well-known cure for many ills prescribed in famous sanitariums in Switzerland. We were too poor to see a doctor when the flu, colds or childhood diseases struck. Mother stuck us into a sweat bath, gave us a cup of steaming herb tea with honey and put a wet compress or sock around our sore throats. I did the same with my five children, and I still treat myself with nature's aids and see a doctor only when it is a serious matter or for a physical checkup. Such habits are good for your overworked doctor, for your pocketbook and your health.

Drugs never cure a body. Your body has to fight and overcome ills of any kind by itself, and all we can do is aid and strengthen our systems to do so. Sometimes, drugs do aid and antibiotics have saved many lives, but the same medicines have killed others because they were used at the wrong time. I believe that a loving God grew a different healing herb for any sickness that can befall us. We just haven't discovered all of them because we don't try very hard.

Water is essential if our bodies are to heal themselves. Health authorities will tell us that we need a glass of water per ten pounds of our body weight per day. Oh, dear! Could you at

34

least settle for one glass per twenty pounds? Your body might like more as time goes by, but something is better than nothing. At least start to drink; your kidneys might smile and your scale will groan less. Contrary to popular belief, you do not gain weight from drinking water but from eating too much of the wrong food.

You say, "I don't have a problem with getting enough liquid. I drink many cups of coffee a day, but I still feel lousy."

Try the coffee-water without the coffee. And put something less strong into the water, like fresh lemon or lime, herbs of your choice, fruit juice, weak black tea, honey in place of sugar, and drink it between meals, not with the meal.

Coffee keeps you from burning calories and so from losing weight. It also can make you jumpy, nervous and terribly depressed, as it does me. I have a low blood sugar problem and any stimulant plays havoc with my body chemistry and my moods.

You say, "I don't care if I die earlier, but I want what I want when I want it."

Well, I am not so concerned about dying as about the way I die. I can't believe that God wants us to die inch by inch, or drop dead prematurely. Heart attacks can leave a vacuum behind that will bring nothing but hardship to the living and perhaps a question on God's face: "My child, how come you are at My door before your time? I assigned a task for you to do which someone else now has to take on his over-burdened shoulders."

It is not always God's perfect will when people fall sick or die. More often it is a natural consequence of our thoughtless habits and foolish behavior. Our body is the temple of the Holy Spirit. Do we dare to neglect what God himself wants to use? (See 1 Corinthians 3:16; 6:19,20.) If we do take care of ourselves for Him, He will return our sensible efforts by giving us a happier, fuller life.

I do much praying and asking about God's will for my

35

health. I am not preoccupied with it, but I do ask Him to remind me and nudge me whenever my spirit is willing, but the flesh unwilling to exercise or get a drink. I do not only need an able body now to serve the Lord better, but for the stormy future when it will be much more difficult to live in ease and plenty.

You may say, "I'll live it up now and do as I please. I'll reform my ways when times get hard. I'll lose weight when I have to, not before."

My friend, the time when you "have to" lose weight may be when you can get no food. Starvation is never a good way to lose weight, even in times when you are not under the stress of actual survival. I know that because I have been there. You don't ever get in shape and stay there by a crash diet of any sort—neither in good or bad times. We stay or get back to health and a normal figure by meeting our needs as God designed it. And He ordained for us to breathe deeply, to move our muscles, to drink water and eat wisely.

Spend time outdoors. One hour outside, even under an overcast sky, provides important vitamin D, among other things, for your child and you.

Drink enough water to flush every body cell of waste matters, otherwise you become stagnant and susceptible to disease germs and viruses.

Learn also to eat right and to handle stress by finding healthful relaxation.

I believe that every city dweller should have access to some simple camping and picnic equipment and we should get back to nature whenever possible. It might take effort and bring sand, dirt and extra work, but it is worth it. We need to come back to God's way of living. I have a deep conviction anyway that God's children should not live in inner cities unless God needs them there. In turbulent times the big cities have always been the hardest place to survive, physically and emotionally. Children can be raised easier in the simple environment of smaller towns.

I sometimes have a flash of a vision of what will happen if inflation increases and welfare checks are not adequate to buy enough food for the hungry. Or if a famine or a labor strike brings a food shortage, even for a few weeks. Riots, looting, violence and crime will run wild, mostly in the big cities.

Your own backyard might cause you to gripe now because you have to mow and water it although your heart and muscles wonder why you complain when the work outside is good for you. But I have seen people stay on top and avoid damage to their health and their families because they found a small square of soil to grow food to supplement a monotonous war diet. In Europe, many city people own or lease a little garden outside the city where they spend much of their free time. During the last war these *schreber garten* saved many lives.

I did not always own a backyard myself. And right now I travel too much to take care of any garden or lawn. But God has always opened the way for me to get out every so often into nature and away from the city and the terrible smog.

When the children were growing up, we took them camping, to the beach, hiking, and I always kept our camp stove intact and warm sleeping bags and enough provisions in the cupboards to see us through in case of a blackout, earthquake or other emergency. My children would tease me because I always anticipated trouble and was prepared for it. But I would prefer not to ever need my emergency provisions than to be caught once again without water or a way to heat some food when gas and electricity are knocked out, or extra blankets in freezing weather. It's hard enough to be caught yourself, but to watch children suffer or go hungry is worse, especially if they are your own.

I presently live in the city because God needs me here right now. He has given me a way out of the city in our little motor home. I travel much in it and I believe it is not a luxury. Right now it provides restful travel for relaxation and a touch with

37

nature that I need. Tomorrow, it could become a refuge when I might have to flee into the country in case of city turmoil.

I have some other deep convictions. I believe every family member should have a bicycle. It's not only great exercise in good times but maybe a lifesaver when gas stations are without gas or many thoroughfares jammed with cars carrying panicked people trying to get away. You can get a long way from trouble on a bicycle even if you must lift it over rubble or ruins. And in case of war, we might have to get out and around destroyed freeways or streets.

What do such dark statements have to do with the topic of a healthy body? I pray we never have to face what only clouds our horizon at the present time. But if war or other disaster hits, we can't ignore it; we must face it! If you are in good shape, you will make it. And if you are not, you might or might not. You could end up permanently damaged in soul and body until it's time for you to be with the Lord, maybe several years later. Such a thing can happen under normal circumstances too, if you do not have a healthy body.

What unnecessary suffering many of God's children bring upon themselves and their families because they do not follow the Spirit's gentle nudging toward sensible, healthful living now.

So, you are going to do something about the matter tomorrow? You'll never do it unless you start today. And tomorrow it might be too late.

"Beloved, I pray that in all respects you may prosper and be in good health, just as your soul prospers" (3 John 2, *NASB*).

Take the time and effort to write down in your notebook both your immediate and your far-reaching plans for each of the areas: clean air; pure water and food; good exercise.

6. *Our Daily Bread*

What did the good Lord mean when He taught us to pray, "Give us this day our daily bread" (Matthew 6:11)?

My favorite Bible scholar explains (in a German dissertation) that the original text in the Aramaic, the language in which Jesus spoke and taught, reads: Our bread for tomorrow, give us today! In ancient Hebrew and Aramaic the word, *machar* means not only the next day but any time in the future, even the end of time. Consequently Jesus, in His prayer, did not include only the bread for one day, but future bread and the Bread of Life which we need now and forever. It makes more sense to believe that Jesus thought of bread for our spirit and soul and not for our body alone; and not only for today, but for every day, until we are with Him in the heavenly kingdom to eat at His table (see Matthew 26:29).

Our need for spiritual bread should be our *first* concern, but we are human enough to always worry about our physical bread first. God understands our weaknesses and fears and He reassures us (see Matthew 6:25,26).

At the present time, America does not have too many people who have to worry where the next meal will come from. But inflation has caused a shift of diet in many homes because the grocery bill has become a major budget item. I remember when we came to America in 1955, my food allowance for two adults and two children was $12 a week. My husband earned 95¢ per hour on a construction job. His paycheck got larger as he found better jobs, but so did our family. I always had to watch every penny to make ends meet. I got into the habit of praying whenever I went grocery shopping. I always thanked the Lord that I was allowed to live in a land that had enough food to feed everybody, and I asked for wisdom to get the best food value, and what would help us most to stay well, with the money I had to spend. I still pray the same prayer today. Now, the children have grown and are either eating in college cafeterias or doing their own cooking. And I bring home much smaller grocery sacks—but pay more for two people than I once did for all of us.

I do not foresee in the near future a time of starvation for America, though prices are rising without an end in sight. And a future war could touch our continent although we have not had any physical war-conflict on United States soil for the last century. Atomic warfare or prolonged drought could cause great upsets.

My present concern is not the absence of food, but the quality of it. Americans are overfed but undernourished. The various sicknesses resulting from this condition are often disguised as illnesses without visible cause. But we simply are often as healthy as we eat.

There are big discussions about what is healthy or harmful and sometimes the big food industries can manipulate government administrators and "fix" research to favor their products. In the confusing labyrinth of opinions I have checked food values against one simple principle: How close to the way *God grew it* does it come to me? The more refined, bleached, powdered, pre-digested, colored and pre-cooked it is the less I trust it for building my body. I might taste it here and there for a nice treat, but for daily food I stick with whole grains, legumes, fresh or frozen vegetables, fresh or dried fruit, fresh lean meats (mainly fish and fowl), unsaturated oils, milk in soured form (cottage cheese, buttermilk, yoghurt, mild cheese), fresh eggs and natural sweeteners like honey, maple syrup, molasses and fructose (sugar often used for diabetic problems).

I followed my basic principle even when I had very little money to feed seven members of the family. And I found that it worked well for us.

I believe that one can easily pay in doctor bills what he tries to save in food money. The cheapest food is not always the most economical buy in the long run.

My greatest complaint has always been the daily *bread*— literally. Perhaps you heard me say before, that one of the first English words I understood when we came to America was "Wonder Bread." It made sense to me to call it that; it was a total wonder to me how people could exist on it. I still wonder the same thing now, only more so.

The main foods provided by God on this globe for the human race are various grains. The Western world uses wheat, rye and corn. The Orient lives on rice. God knew well what He did when He designed the *whole* kernels of grain and He put just the right proportions of bran, germ, oil, vitamins, minerals and the inner white carbohydrates (we call it flour) together, to serve our bodily needs. Along comes man to "improve" God's work and we take off the bran, the wheat germ, the brown shell which carries the lifegiving vitamins and minerals and use only the refined inner white part to produce a "better" bread. Of course, we add a few vitamins and minerals again after we robbed the flour of *every* nutrient (except the empty calories) for the body. If someone took $100 out of your pocket and gave you 100 pennies back,

41

would you let him get away with it? We let the food industries get away with a lot more. And the refined foods are the great culprits which cause the severe problems of overweight and deficiency diseases in us and our children.

/ If God meant for us to eat white sponges for bread He would have grown it that way. He intended for us to eat carbohydrates *together with* the right balance of roughage, vitamins, minerals and fats.

I am not a food faddist and I don't advertise unbalanced fads of any kind; but it is common knowledge that we Americans eat too much refined foods, made from white flour and white sugar. The rice is polished and the breakfast cereals processed to death by heat, chemicals, sugar, colors and artificial flavors. Even commercial baby foods are not much better, and they include too much sugar and/or salt.

How do I dare to say such things? I taught home economics while teaching high school dropouts here in America and I have read bulletins and seen food value statistics that never reach your kitchen.

Leading magazines have begun lately to educate the public that lack of roughage food is believed to encourage intestinal cancer. I knew that fact before I came to America in 1955. Shortly before we left Europe, I read the report of a cancer congress in Sweden where the leading scientists of the world had met to compare their findings. One of the surprising facts they all had in common was that nearly every cancer victim they had treated showed a record of prolonged constipation.

Now I am waiting to see when someone will have the courage to try to tell the American public that white flour and sugar are grave health dangers, too. It took many years for the government to prove that cigarettes are a killer, and the findings came too late for many lung cancer patients. I pray they will research the harmful effects of refined sugar and other carbohydrates next.

A German study after World War II showed an interesting

statistical curve. During the war the German rate of heart disease and cancer dropped sharply. After the war the curve of these killers began to rise again. And it rose in the *exact* proportion to the sugar consumption of the German public.

You say, "What can we do about it?"

As in spiritual or soul matters, changes in physical habits take time and effort. If you and your children are used to eating white bread and lots of white noodles, rice or sweet foods, it will take a re-education of your taste buds. You will have to learn to chew again, if you want your stomach to handle the rougher consistency of whole grain breads, crisp salads, under-cooked vegetables, unpolished rice, etc. You'll find that the body needs a lot less when you switch to a more natural diet. This makes up for higher prices or extra effort. I did most of my bread baking myself while the children were home and I prefer multigrain to whole wheat bread because it provides better proteins than wheat alone. However, whole wheat, sprouted wheat or whole rye bread is better than any white bread.

Cancer research in Europe ties food deficiency and certain foods needed as preventatives close together. Prevention of any sickness is always easier than trying to cure the illness.

We don't know exactly what causes cancer, but we do know that whatever it is, it and other grave illnesses can attack the body only when the body cells are weakened. Keeping ourselves in good shape and our immunities intact renders hostile viruses and bad germs powerless. The body can destroy them and flush them out. God in His loving care laid healing into the foods and herbs. He gave us, after death came as a result of sin, this answer for the human race (see Genesis 9:3; Psalm 104:10-15).

It is interesting to me that modern health research is finding more and more that God's natural ways of growing, preparing and preserving food are the safest and best ways after all. Primitive cultures grind and bake the grain as needed, day by day. Now it has been discovered that freshly ground and baked grain carries the highest vitamin content.

Breakfast cereals are richest if cooked and served whole —the pioneers' cornmush, grits, or oats were not so dumpy after all. Neither was their way of harvesting, cooking and eating the sweet corn straight from the garden to the table.

The leaven of ancient or primitive baking is the sour dough. Souring vegetables was, besides drying or smoking, the only way to preserve and store food for the non-growing seasons.

European cancer research has found that building up the natural acidity of our intestinal tract encourages good digestion, brings about regular bowel movements and destroys infections, strengthens weakened cells and builds up immunity or represses the forming of new tumors after cancer surgery. Natural acidity can be provided with the acidophilus bacteria found in yoghurt, buttermilk, cottage cheese, sauerkraut and other naturally soured vegetables, sour dough, etc.

Countries like Bulgaria know little or no cancer. What do they eat? Dark rye bread, much yoghurt, plenty of cabbage, onions, garlic and green peppers, sweet paprika and other vegetables and fruit they grow. They report little tooth decay and their people stay strong and live to be ninety and a hundred years old! We have the same report from the Hunzas and other little countries who have not yet been "blessed" by the improvements and the refined life-style of modern Western civilization. None of these isolated cultures show our degenerative diseases or obesity.

I often tell overweight people who ask my counsel that it takes more than a few weeks of half starvation to stay slim and healthy. It has to be a change of life-style. As we turn around in spirit and soul, we sometimes forget that God wants to sanctify all, not only part of us. This means our body needs God's renewal, too. I always hesitate when people ask me to outline a diet program for them. I believe the Lord can do it for His children, and do it to meet individual needs, better than I can.

I don't encourage extremes. God told us to be moderate in all things (see 1 Corinthians 9:25). People can go overboard in any direction, and too much of a good thing can be as harmful as something bad.

Vegetarianism can be an excellent way of life, if people study it carefully and find enough *complete* proteins for their diet. But too often a meatless diet tries to make up for animal protein by too many sweets. And vegetarians are not necessarily protected from cancer or high blood pressure either. It takes God's wisdom and our willing, open minds to go the course the Lord sees best for our personal need or the demands of our family.

I will never forget what someone said to me after I had given a lecture on nutrition in a retreat and recommended to the listeners to ask God for His will in their daily lives. A young mother came to me and bubbled over with excitement of how she would exercise and start to eat a decent breakfast and so forth. She ended up by saying, "The only thing I am not willing yet to ask Him about is my sugar intake. I love sweets, candy bars, ice cream, doughnuts and pralines."

"Why don't you dare to ask the Lord about it?" I asked gently.

"Because I know what He will show me," she said with a laugh. "He has already tried to show it to me before I heard you, but I simply am not ready to listen yet!"

In eating, drinking, living and sleeping it boils down to the same issue after all, doesn't it? Is Jesus Christ your Lord in *all* things, or are you holding on to something that you are unwilling to give up?

We look down with great superiority on those who are "hooked" by drugs, tobacco, alcohol or other evangelical taboos. If Satan cannot hook us with unacceptable things, he'll try to hold us in bondage with the acceptable way of life.

Anything that forcibly holds us—be it a habit, food, drink or even compulsory overwork for God's cause—is not in God's will for us. He gave us freedom to choose and to choose wisely.

The best of everything comes to those who let the Lord choose for them. He knows us best. He made us. He knows what we need, but He will never force us to do His will. If we obey Him, we don't do it for His sake, as we so often think; we do it for our sake. God never asks us to sacrifice or give up anything unless He can replace it with something better and richer.

Try it! You might like it, after all.

The decision is up to you. What do you intend to do about your eating habits? Don't just think about it, write it down, then do it.

Healthful food I will eat:

7. Questions I Have Been Asked

Question: *What will happen if inflation increases? What will happen to our money?*

Answer: I am not a prophet. But, according to well-known economists, the inflation spiral of the dollar has gone beyond the point of return, so inflation will increase and eat up our savings and buying power. I believe that it will take a miracle of God to reverse the trend and heal the nation's finances. God is eager to do so if we do our part as outlined in 2 Chronicles 7:14. "If my people, which are called by my name, shall humble themselves, and pray, and seek my face, and turn from their wicked ways; then will I hear from heaven, and will forgive their sin, and heal their land."

If we don't do it soon, we have two directions to go: either we lose our present standard of currency altogether and start all over with a new monetary system or we end up in total government control and socialism to the point where our large industrial free enterprises—oil companies, utilities, mining and transportation systems, etc.—become nationalized and government owned. Both directions will alter our present way of life, our form of government and will strangle our freedom. Twice I have seen the value of money vanish in Germany. After World War I in the 1920s the people went to buy a loaf of bread with a wheelbarrow full of money.

After World War II the *reichsmark* again lost its total value and every German started out with forty new German *marks*. Today, the West German *mark* is stable because the West German government does not permit the printing of more and more paper money which has no backing.

This inflationary money is what is happening right now in the United States and it has brought on our great national debt. The floating paper money exceeds its worth because the dollar is off the gold standard, and we have no other standard or limitation in its place. This can only lead to a money crash if it is not reversed. Otherwise, it will stop itself by ultimately becoming worthless.

A nation can survive such drastic measures but it brings hardship and severe living conditions, similar to the depression the United States went through after the stock market crash. It's not pleasant but people can come out of it if they have the inner and physical strength to bounce back. Christians should be able to show others the way if or when it happens.

Question: How do you invest your money at the present time? Is there a way to beat inflation or the total loss of our savings? **Answer:** I don't save money right now. All my income from royalties and speaking goes into the ministry. I figure my account is safest in God's hands. When times get rough, I just ask God to send me what I need. I'd rather spend my money now to reach America with my message before it is too late than watch it go to waste later.

However, not everybody wants or needs to take such action. If you have savings, consider the following: Economists suggest that the safest investment is gold, diamonds or property. I would buy land if I ever had some extra money, and buy it outside of the big cities. If the property has water and soil to grow food on it, it is always a good investment. On this property, I would aim toward self-sufficiency by digging a well and using wind and solar power to provide alternate utilities for living quarters.

If I owned a place in the city I would mortgage it and buy a small country place for cash, so that nobody could take my property away when the dollar dies. I would use the inflated money of the next few years to pay off all debts, so that I owned everything I would need to survive. Records show that in both places—in the United States during the depression and in Europe during the monetary crash—banks foreclosed on properties which were almost paid for. That's where the lenders gained the most. So it makes sense to either own completely or carry a mortgage where the bank has a bigger share in it than you.

It is never wise to be without cash reserves to float in case of illness, unemployment or other emergencies. But if I had more than that reserve available, I would buy now what I need or want for the future. That's what I am doing anyway. I pay cash to avoid all the extra carrying charges and I am getting what I know I will need to be comfortable in times of over-charges or scarcity. If you know your car will fall apart shortly, it is wise to find an economical decent vehicle now. If your mattress is bad for your back, replace it. Next year or two years from now, you might pay much more and get less. The dollar has lost 50% of its value since 1967. Economists predict it will be cut by another 50% by the early eighties.

Don't put yourself into deep debt, but don't delay your purchases to gain interest on your savings, either. The inflation moves faster than your bank benefits.

Just ask God! I do much praying and let the Lord even do my shopping in areas other than food. He will do it for you if you let Him.

Question: *Some people store food. Should Christians store up for the future or can we just trust God?*

Answer: I believe that every household should have at all times enough reserves in the home to last at least from two to four weeks. This is wise in case of disaster, labor strikes or a sudden job layoff. The staples should be able to keep without electricity or gas, in case of blackouts or strikes in the utility productions.

When I last spoke in England, I saw electricity turned off and on without warning because of strikes. Even hospitals never knew when it would happen, sometimes in the middle of surgery. We can anticipate similar problems when things get more and more expensive. Labor will protest!

Wheat keeps indefinitely if it is stored correctly. Milk and other protein powders keep for years in airtight cans. So does honey, legumes and other food-stretchers. Freeze-dried food or dried fruit stays well too. But none of those things do any good unless you learn to use them now. You should also use the rotation method, especially in canned goods. I always buy big packages or cans of the items I consistently use and I keep at least one in reserve. When I use the reserve, I replace it. I do that not only with my basic foods, but with soap, toilet paper, sanitary napkins, toothpaste, shampoo, razor blades, skin creams, and any other thing that would cause an inconvenience if I had to do without it for weeks. People who need regular medication, like diabetics or those with bad hearts, should never run out to the last dosage before getting a new prescription. That advice is sensible even in the best of times.

If one has the money and knows or learns how to use stored food, you cannot lose by stocking up now. Food will become more and more expensive; as the meat prices rise, we all should learn how to stretch our daily meals with whole grains, sprouts, and healthful fillers like barley, lentils, dried green peas, cracked wheat, oats, corn and other basics which will meet our family's taste and need. If you store grain, have on hand a little hand mill in addition to your electric grinder. Water is good for a long time if it is bottled spring or distilled

50

water. Some people keep their water reserves in a water bed. If you do that, have a small water washer handy to purify it before you use it. Here again the Lord has to show us individually what needs to be done.

I believe there is a difference between carelessness and demonstrating "faith," between sensible foresight and spending wildly on foolish things. If we ever needed God's wisdom, it is now. We must never cry wolf or become doomsday prophets before it is time. But we must warn the people around us before it is too late. Christ knows that harsh times are coming and the Lord is willing to show us how to prepare ourselves at all three levels. After we do all we can, then we must relax and leave all else to the Lord. He is able to meet any emergency for us.

Question: What about the energy crisis? Do you think that a gasoline shortage and other problems will plague us again? Answer: I don't need to be a prophet to answer that. Yes, we can look for a lot more problems when it comes to energy. We simply have a shortage, not of resources, but of energy production. Crude oil is not the only energy resource. We have plenty of natural gas, coal, oil shale, uranium and geothermal energy for hundreds of years, but we must find new ways to utilize what we have here in the United States in raw form. That will take time and effort and somebody in our government should have prepared for the present crisis ten years ago. They knew it was coming, but it was so much easier to ignore it than to risk political suicide by suggesting unpopular measures.

Our country again has two directions to go. Either we can price energy products so high that people will use them sparingly or we can ration them, paying a bit less, but having no guarantee they will be available when we need them most, especially in the winter. I believe every home should have a small heating unit which can keep one room warm when gas or electricity are turned off or heating oil is so expensive that you can't afford to heat the whole house by it. A small coal or wood-burner stove is ideal. Put it in front of the open fireplace. A fireplace wastes too much heat and wood anyway.

As big gasoline guzzling cars don't sell well anymore, so will big homes become hard to sell in a few years. People will not be able to afford utilities for heating and cooling—whether they are priced high or rationed. If I owned a big home, I would start now to add solar equipment and do a good job installing insulation against heat or cold. You will be much more snug in such a home and it will also have great sales values when you want to sell.

The time of waste is over and we all have to learn to deal with increasing shortages. Other lands have done it for a long time. And if you can use solar energy, you pay for the installation and upkeep, but not for the source of energy. I trust that nobody will charge us for the use of sunshine. God gave sunshine and rain free to the righteous and unrighteous (see Matthew 5:45). It is smart to be alert and to show an interest in new developments, such as solar and wind power. And again ask God to guide you. He will!

Right now I am watching with interest the new models of motor homes which run not only on gasoline but also on propane. Since I'll need such transportation for my work, I am praying that God will help the manufacturers to develop such new services. I love my crock pot and little microwave oven. Anything which saves energy has my interest. Who knows, you might see me someday pedal across the country on a bicycle to attend a meeting. I don't care what it takes, I intend to keep my schedule.

Question: *You say so often that you see every symptom of Nazi Germany raise its ugly head here in America. What do you see?*

Answer: No type of dictatorship or any kind of "ism" (socialism, communism, etc.) can get a foothold in a democracy unless the people forget the meaning of freedom. When people want to exchange the insecurity of freedom for the security of government handouts, and responsibility of individual decision-making for blaming others for all the failures, we are ready for takeover.

Since political freedom is built on our personal freedom of choice and the inner control of responsible individual citizens, it takes courage to be free. Freedom involves risks because we have to think and act for ourselves. Since nobody is perfect, we have to admit when we make a mistake and take the responsibility for it, even the consequences!

When our society wants or loves anything more than God and freedom, we will lose freedom. And the truth we do not realize is that, if we give up freedom for comfort, pleasure or security, we shall lose those things together with the freedom we relinquished.

America is at the brink now where people are willing to give up what they have to be assured of a guaranteed income. The satanic powers are at work undermining the thinking process of the people, especially our youth.

The media as a whole favors liberal views, glorifies sin and encourages us to see "different" as "better." And the values of the last two hundred years are put down as "outdated" and "old fashioned." Hitler did that! His media brainwashed the German people to the point that they followed him like sheep to the slaughterhouse.

Brainwashing is a simple process. Someone presents an idea long enough until it is believed by most people. The free press of the Western world is increasingly doing just that. We receive only one side of the news and the government picks false scapegoats for problems created by the red-tape monster. The Nazis picked the Jews to blame all evil on. Likewise, the United States has indicated that the oil crisis is Israel's fault; actually growing government controls are the

53

true culprit. Government control chokes individual initiative and free enterprise. Our political leaders meddle with personal lives, yes, even the spark of life itself. I see the same trends Hitler had in medicine, education, military planning, economy (paper money without backing) and ideology. And all of it is a reverse of what made America special and great.

In the religious realm the Judeo-Christian inner control, which has always been the foundation of our freedom, is questioned, shaken and replaced by "new" forms of meditation. I don't care what it is called, if it has certain characteristics, it is the same occult the Nazis had. And it is dangerous to political and individual freedom of choice. These are the makings of satanic ideology:

1. Vain repetitions in place of meaningful prayer. See Matthew 6:7.

2. Emptying the mind to allow "something" to float in. God never floats in. He enters after He is asked in specific terms and invited in. See Revelation 3:20.

3. Good "feelings" and a temporary sense of physical "highs" as a result of such meditation. See 2 Corinthians 11:14.

4. Reduced willpower to make clear choices. A vague willingness to see good in everything. See Deuteronomy 30:19,20.

5. A strong irritability, anger and aggressiveness when the hailed benefits of the new meditation forms are challenged. See John 3:19-21.

6. A denial of Jesus Christ as the Saviour of the world and the Son of God. See 1 John 4:1-3; John 3:16-18.

7. Increased interest in drugs, hypnotizing music, fortune-telling, witchcraft, superstition and horoscopes. All of these are an abomination to the God of the Bible. See Deuteronomy 18:9-13.

Can you now see what I see? Pray and ask God for His Spirit of discernment and freedom within yourself.

Question: *Will you share some of your very personal philosophies and tips for daily living with us?*
Answer: My life centers around God and His ministry for our land, and my children.

When I wake up in the morning, I tell Jesus that I love Him. He is my Husband and I treat Him just like that. I ask every day for the mind of Christ, His Spirit and love and that I might learn to trust Him completely. I say, "Don't just help me, Jesus; please do it for me." Too often we are tempted to plan our day and then say hurriedly to God, "Please bless *my* plans!" I ask God to make my plans fail if they are not His will for my life because He knows best.

When I cannot sleep at night or I wake up before morning, I immediately ask, "Do You want to talk to me or I to You, Lord? Did You waken me?" Sometimes it is God who wants to show me something which I cannot comprehend in the hustle of the day; sometimes it is my worried heart or mind, stirred by some evil fears. If it is the latter, I rebuke Satan and ask God to give me back my sleep. Until it happens I pray or think about God's promises. It works better than any sleeping pill.

My body is at its lowest in the morning. I have always been a slow starter. My best pep pill is the shower. Nothing wakes me better than changing the water temperature of the shower three times. I start good and warm, switch to cold (lately to "cool" as I get older); switch back to warmer than before, back to cold; once more to hot, so that my skin turns pink, and finish with cold. I rub myself dry with a rough towel to make my body tingle and my blood circulate. Five times, I fought pregnancy's morning sickness successfully by using this method.

I drink some cups of hot herb tea with fresh lemon. My favorite teas are rose hips, red clover, chamomile, peppermint, jasmine, fennel, or some prepared mixtures. This is my first intake. Then I eat a fruit (apples are my favorite), some

55

yoghurt, an egg and a piece of whole grain toast. Breakfast is a must to stay slim and well!

When I feel a cold or infection coming on, I take a sweat bath and, every two hours, drink more herb tea while chewing or taking vitamin C in heavier doses than usual. I also increase my intake of Golden Seal capsules. I usually shake what "bugs" me within twenty-four hours.

For my children, I used the bathtub for every illness they had. I put a feverish child into a pleasantly warm bath and while he drank his favorite tea or hot lemon water with honey, I added hot water slowly to the tub while pouring bath water over his chest and back and shoulders with a big cup. Children love to be fussed over. As soon as I saw little sweat beads under his nose or on his forehead, I knew I had the fever broken; so I unplugged the tub and when it was empty, I poured cool (never cold) water over every part of his body. Then I rubbed his skin, except his face, with moistened salt and rinsed it off with more lukewarm water. After rubbing his body dry with a rough towel, I put the child back under cool sheets and massaged his whole body with a gentle baby oil or cream. I have broken many a sickness with this and other such water treatments. I consider water one of God's greatest therapeutics against germs and ills.

I fight depression with water, too! Whenever I hit one of my deep miserable blues, I check, "Is my blood sugar low?" I have hypoglycemia and one of the great curses of it is depression and fearful apprehensions without specific reasons. I get myself some cups of relaxing tea, eat some protein, and stay off all carbohydrates, even honey or whole grains, until I feel better. I go for a brisk walk or into the shower if I possibly can. I make myself do something positive like write some encouraging letters to others who ask for help or I call a person who needs to know that someone cares (though I dislike telephones). I never allow myself to voice my negative fears and feelings. I talk hope when I "feel" defeat. I write about the victory when I wonder if my prayers go above the ceiling.

Our words, inspired by the Spirit and commanded by our will (not our black moods), can reverse our emotions. If we talk illness and depression, we shall be ill and down. If we talk faith and know we can trust God because He said so and not because we feel it, we come out of the black fog to a better tomorrow. At least I do.

I stay wide open to learn new things every day and make it a point not to fall into a rut. I deliberately change daily routines to stay flexible and young. After all, everybody is as young or old as he wishes to be. And I am aiming for another time of youth since the Nazis stole mine. God said I could. He has promised to make up the years the locusts have eaten (see Joel 2:25).

Is there anything you want out of life you haven't gotten? Ask Jesus for it. He said that He'll give us the desires of our heart (see Psalm 37:4).

Question: Could you share some of your favorite food tips and recipes with us?
Answer: I believe in taking vitamins, added minerals and herb pills because the soil often is depleted and even the fresh grown food or fruit is deficient in expected vitamins and trace elements.

For my sore joints, I take, three times daily, a handful of alfalfa tablets. It is one of the best things to prevent or ease arthritis.

I regularly take multiple vitamins, vitamins A and E in capsules. Besides these and mineral combinations I add zinc, calcium with vitamin D, potassium, pantothenic acid, lecithin, PABA, and time-released vitamin C. Golden Seal capsules and garlic mixed with parsley in pill form are infection fighters. And I am prone to any bug that comes along on my travels and contacts with so many people.

Don't think you must take exactly what I take. You should

ask God to show you what *you* need. Some have a strong physical constitution; I have very frail health and need to be alert to my body's signals or I cannot keep up my strenuous schedule. I ask God to pick what I need and He does and provides the money for it. Natural vitamins are expensive, but I have very few doctor bills.

If you want to learn how to bake whole-grain bread, start with my fast spoonbread:

/ ***Spoonbread***

Mix with a big spoon:
1 cup white flour with
1 cup warm water and
1 cup buttermilk, yoghurt, sour milk, canned or reconstituted dry or whole milk with
1 pkg dry or active yeast (not food yeast you might take for vitamin B) and
1 tbsp sugar and
3 tbsp honey or molasses

Set aside and let it rise a bit in a warm place. If need be, put the dough into the unheated oven on the upper rack with a bowl of hot water on the lower rack. When it shows some bubbly consistency, mix into it:
1 tbsp salt
1 egg
3 tbsp oil
2½ cups whole wheat or mixed grain flour

If it is still very sticky and wet (flour consistency varies) add up to another cup of white flour to make a smooth, moist dough. Spoon into a bread pan or a large empty juice can or two which you have greased well with a hard shortening like margarine, butter or Crisco, and dusted with flour to prevent sticking. Let the dough rise in a warm place until it is one-third or double in bulk. Bake for 10 minutes at 450° then lower the temperature to 350° and bake for 35–40 minutes more. Take out of pan or can and let it cool before you cut it.

After you get the idea how breadbaking works, find some nice recipes for kneaded bread and try them. If you work, put the bread for the second rising into the refrigerator overnight or during your working hours. It rises much slower but is ready to bake when you are. If you freeze yeast dough, you must let it defrost slowly and let it rise again like fresh dough.

Sometimes I use a simple bread dough with some added sweeteners and the grated rind of a lemon as a base for streuselkuchen.

Streuselkuchen

Spread the dough as thin as possible on a greased cookie sheet. Your oiled fingers work best. Let it rise. Cover it with slices of fresh apples or pears or Italian plums or a fruit marmalade. Make a crumb mixture of flour or oatmeal, some brown sugar, fructose, butter or margarine, lemon rind and vanilla to suit your own taste. Sprinkle the crumbs over the fruit and bake it quickly to a golden brown, at 400° to 450°. Like pizza, the thicker the bottom dough, the lower the heat and the longer the baking.

Play with yeast dough for buns and other breads. Nothing smells or tastes better than mother's fresh-baked wholesome goodies. Add a stew or soup and a crisp salad and you have a meal. If you goof, try again. Don't give up if your first try isn't perfect. I have fed some of my mishaps to the birds.

I also make banana or date and nut breads and put the dough into paper muffin cups and bake them as muffins. Wrap them up in little plastic baggies and freeze them. I reheat as many as needed for a meal. I keep all my cut bread in the freezer, since the kids are gone, and take one slice out at a time to toast it.

Banana Bread

Mix with a fork:
¼ cup oil
¼ cup honey

Fructose as it suits your taste
3 tbsp brown sugar
1 egg
2–3 tbsp yoghurt or milk or water
1 tsp vanilla or rum flavor
1 tsp salt
½ tsp soda
    Add to it
2 fork-mashed bananas
1 cup bran
½ to 1 cup chopped nuts
1 to 1½ cups flour mixed with
2 tsp baking powder. (The amount of flour depends on the type used.)

Mix to a consistency that you can drop by big spoonfuls into paper muffin cups. Bake at 350° for 35–45 minutes.

Try other quick breads like date-nut, raisin-cinnamon, etc. Add flax seed, rice polishings, wheat germ, dried fruit. Use your God-given imagination.

Don't take it personally if your family doesn't like new things the very first time you serve them.

If you try to serve more nutritious breakfasts and the family demands its customary commercial cereals, enrich them with sprinkled wheat germ or your own sprouted wheat.

I sprout wheat by putting the grain in my wide-mouthed thermos bottle. Cover it with warm, not hot, water and let it soak for twenty to thirty hours, exchanging the warm water when it no longer smells fresh.

Then rinse the wheat good with warm water and put it without water into an empty bowl lined with crumpled tissue into a place that provides even warmth: a yoghurt maker, a warm water bottle or in an unheated oven near the pilot light. I serve it as soon as the first white sprout tips appear. It smells and tastes pleasantly sour, due to the acidophilus stage of the germination. That's when your body can get the best use out of it.

I also use my widemouthed thermos bottle to precook cereal like cracked wheat, millet, brown rice and other grain. I pour boiling water over it. *Never* screw the top shut, but put it lightly on top. The bottle might pop if you screw the top tightly. Let it sit overnight. Next morning it takes only short minutes to prepare the breakfast.

Grain also cooks itself if you let it come to a boil and set it overnight on the pilot light.

Granola is good to eat if you have no time to cook.

Where there is a will, there is a way. We can usually do what we really want to do.

As a summary to this final chapter, we are asking you to write some answers for us, not for you alone.

Would you take the time to fill out the questionnaire and give us an idea how to help you more in the future.

Questionnaire

	YES	NO
Has this little book given you some needed information?	____	____
Do you believe we should prepare more detailed information and research for a larger book?	____	____

Which topics would interest you most?

Nutrition and recipes	____
Food storage	____
Investments	____
Money matters	____
Home improvements	____
Sales tips for real estate	____
Tips on buying land	____
Health care	____
Solar energy	____
Spiritual aid	____
Mental aid	____
Emotional aid	____
Physical aid	____

Is there a subject you truly want to know about such as: child rearing; teenage problems; other suggested topics? _____

Do you have some good ideas of your own to share? If so, we cannot guarantee that we can include all of them in a future book. But if we do, we will give you credit by name—unless you request anonymity.

Will you please become involved and at least check our questionnaire and mail it to us?

HANSI MINISTRIES, INC.
P.O. Box 552, Huntington Beach, CA 92648